FROM THE FILMS OF

Harry Potter
STICKER ART PUZZLES

THUNDER BAY
P·R·E·S·S
San Diego, California

Thunder Bay Press
An imprint of Printers Row Publishing Group
9717 Pacific Heights Blvd, San Diego, CA 92121
www.thunderbaybooks.com • mail@thunderbaybooks.com

Printers Row Publishing Group is a division of Readerlink Distribution Services, LLC.
Thunder Bay Press is a registered trademark of Readerlink Distribution Services, LLC.

Correspondence regarding the content of this book should be sent to Thunder Bay Press, Editorial Department,
at the above address.

Thunder Bay Press
Publisher: Peter Norton • Associate Publisher: Ana Parker
Senior Developmental Editor: April Graham • Developmental Editor: Diane Cain
Editor: Jessica Matteson • Senior Product Manager: Kathryn C. Dalby
Production Team: Jonathan Lopes, Rusty von Dyl

Produced by Judy O Productions, Inc.
Author: Gina Gold

ISBN: 978-1-68412-839-6

Printed, manufactured, and assembled in Heshan, China

26 25 24 23 22   4 5 6 7 8

CONTENTS

INTRODUCTION

On his eleventh birthday, an orphan named Harry Potter learned he was a wizard. But he was not just any wizard. He was "The Boy Who Lived," and a scar in the shape of a lightning bolt on his forehead was a reminder of his near demise at the hands of a Dark wizard so evil few dared speak his name. Harry went on to attend Hogwarts School of Witchcraft and Wizardry, where he met the precocious Hermione Granger and a sweet, but mischievous, boy named Ron Weasley. During the trio's years at Hogwarts, they would learn and embrace the exceptional qualities they would need to become skilled wizards and defeat the Dark forces swirling around them. These qualities included: Leadership and Loyalty, Cleverness and Courage, Patience and Empathy, and, most of all, Friendship.

These pages celebrate those qualities, as well as outstanding attributes embodied by Rubeus Hagrid, Professors Albus Dumbledore, Minerva McGonagall, and Severus Snape, and other beloved characters in the Wizarding World. You'll explore the deep bonds of "Friendship" that Harry, Ron, and Hermione formed in their first year at Hogwarts in *Harry Potter and the Sorcerer's Stone*; the "Courage" Harry displayed as he fought off the Basilisk in *Harry Potter and the Chamber of Secrets*; and Hermione's natural aptitude for "Leadership," as she led her friends in search of Voldemort's Horcruxes in *Harry Potter and the Deathly Hallows - Part 1*.

These fifteen challenging sticker puzzles, with more than one hundred pieces each, bring into view favorite moments from the Harry Potter films that illustrate each notable trait. As you work on the puzzles, watch as favorite characters and iconic scenes from all eight Harry Potter films appear before your eyes, piece by piece.

INSTRUCTIONS

Each sticker puzzle features a framed outline of the image you are trying to piece together. Within the outline are geometric spaces that offer hints as to where each sticker goes. You'll find the stickers starting on **page 52**. Apply each one to the corresponding shape in the outline, and watch as Harry, Hermione, Ron, and your other favorite Wizarding World characters appear!

The stickers can be reused in case you make a mistake. If you need a little help, numbered solutions for the puzzles begin on **page 36**.

FRIENDSHIP

> **" If Harry and Ron hadn't come and found me, I'd probably be dead. "**
>
> **— HERMIONE GRANGER**
> *Harry Potter and the Sorcerer's Stone*

Harry, Ron, and Hermione first met on the Hogwarts Express in *Harry Potter and the Sorcerer's Stone*. It did not take long for the overachieving Hermione to wear on Ron's nerves. One day, Ron told his classmates that she was a "nightmare," adding, "No wonder she hasn't got any friends." When Hermione overheard the insults, she spent the afternoon crying in the girls' bathroom. Later that evening at Hallowe'en feast in the Great Hall, Professor Quirrell ran in shouting that there was a dangerous troll in the dungeon. Dumbledore ordered the students to return to their dormitories. Harry and Ron ignored those orders and instead went to search for Hermione, only to find the troll terrorizing her in the bathroom. The trio quickly vanquished the grotesque creature. But when Professors McGonagall, Snape, and Quirrell arrived, they were upset that the Gryffindor students had disobeyed orders and taken on such a dangerous mission. Despite the risk of possible detention, Hermione lied, saying the incident had been all her fault. Harry and Ron were grateful for her act of friendship, and from then on, the three were nearly inseparable.

FRIENDS LIVE IN YOUR HEART

Harry fended off Lord Voldemort by recalling fond memories of his friends and family. "You're the one who is weak. You will never know love or friendship. And I feel sorry for you."

Harry Potter and the Order of the Phoenix

When Harry was trailing in the second task of the Triwizard Tournament, his friend Neville Longbottom offered him Gillyweed to gain an advantage. After taking the plant, Harry was amazed when he sprouted gills, fins, and webbed fingers and could remain underwater for a full hour to complete the task.

Harry Potter and the Goblet of Fire

Locked in his second-story bedroom on Privet Drive and forbidden to leave by the Dursleys, Harry awoke to the sound of a car engine outside his window. To his surprise, it was Ron and his twin brothers George and Fred in a flying Ford Anglia. They had come to rescue their friend Harry.

Harry Potter and the Chamber of Secrets

When Harry needed a date for Professor Slughorn's Christmas party, he could rely on his friend Luna Lovegood for companionship. Although she was a bit odd, Harry was never ashamed to spend time with her—even when she showed up for the party wearing a rather "unique" metallic dress. Luna was kind and compassionate, and that was what mattered most to Harry.

Harry Potter and the Half-Blood Prince

STICKERS ON PAGE 53. SOLUTION ON PAGE 37.

SELFLESSNESS

> **" I've got to finish whatever Dumbledore started, and I don't know where that'll lead me. "**
>
> **— HARRY POTTER**
> *Harry Potter and the Half-Blood Prince*

In the aftermath of Dumbledore's death, Harry, Ron, and Hermione gathered in the Astronomy Tower to make sense of their loss. Harry was wracked with guilt for not having stopped Snape. Harry vowed to continue the dangerous work his beloved teacher had begun. He'd find the Horcruxes, which were the keys to destroying Lord Voldemort. Harry planned to go it alone because he had no intention of putting his friends in harm's way. But Hermione assured Harry that she and Ron would not let him go without them. "You don't really think you can find all those Horcruxes by yourself," she said. "You need us, Harry."

MAGIC HAPPENS WHEN YOU PUT OTHERS FIRST

Harry could have won the second task of the Triwizard Tournament had he simply saved Ron and returned to the lake's surface. But Harry used the precious time he had left to also save his fellow competitor Gabrielle Delacour's sister, Fleur, forfeiting his chance at victory. Harry came in dead last, but he was awarded second place for his act of selflessness.

Harry Potter and the Goblet of Fire

As Lord Voldemort's oppression grew, Harry, Hermione, and Ron were determined to challenge the Ministry of Magic's ban on Defense Against the Dark Arts. Harry devoted his time to teaching his friends the skills they needed to battle Voldemort and his followers.

Harry Potter and the Order of the Phoenix

Harry sacrificed his own life so the piece of the Dark Lord's soul hidden in his body would die with him. Voldemort would then become mortal and could be killed. Finally, Harry, his friends, and the wizarding world would be safe.

Harry Potter and the Deathly Hallows - Part 2

After Harry, Hermione, and Ron decided to search for Voldemort's Horcruxes, Hermione used an Obliviate Charm on her Muggle parents to erase their memories. She wanted to protect them from Voldemort, as well as from the pain of losing her if she failed to return from her dangerous mission.

Harry Potter and the Deathly Hallows - Part 1

TRUSTWORTHINESS

> ❝ I wanted to come back as soon as I left. I just didn't know how to find you. ❞
>
> — RON WEASLEY
>
> *Harry Potter and the Deathly Hallows - Part 1*

Harry, Hermione, and Ron trusted one another with their lives. But even a bond as strong as theirs could be tested. Being best friends with the Boy Who Lived wasn't always easy, as Ron discovered when Harry's name was pulled from the Goblet of Fire. He also grew jealous when he saw Hermione and Harry share a close moment. But beneath Ron's gruff exterior, he was the same kind, sweet boy Harry and Hermione had met on the Hogwarts Express before their first year at Hogwarts. In *Harry Potter and the Deathly Hallows – Part 1*, Ron decided to follow a ball of light from Dumbledore's Deluminator back to Harry and Hermione after they'd all had a terrible argument. Ron succeeded in smashing Salazar Slytherin's Locket, one of the Horcruxes, with the Sword of Gryffindor. When its negative forces consumed him with doubt and insecurity, it was his trust in his friends that gave him the strength to destroy the locket.

IN A WORLD OF DARKNESS, YOU NEED SOMEONE YOU CAN TRUST

Professor Dumbledore tasked Hagrid with delivering infant Harry Potter to the Dursley home for safekeeping until the child was old enough to attend Hogwarts. Professor McGonagall was skeptical whether the half-giant was right for the job, but Dumbledore assured her: "I'd trust Hagrid with my life." Then Hagrid descended from the night sky on a flying motorbike carrying bundled baby Harry in his arms. It was the first time of many that Hagrid would be the boy's trusted guardian.

Harry Potter and the Sorcerer's Stone

Although Sirius Black was an escaped convict accused of murder, he gained Harry's trust by proving that his friendship with Harry's parents had been real. When Sirius was locked up in a jail cell at Hogwarts, Harry and Hermione swooped in riding Buckbeak and rescued Sirius from the Dementors.

Harry Potter and the Prisoner of Azkaban

The Weasleys were the loving family Harry had never known. When the Death Eaters attacked him and his friends, the Weasleys' home, The Burrow, became a logical safe house. Arthur and Molly Weasley and their children could always be trusted to be loving and supportive and to provide a haven for Harry and others in need.

Harry Potter and the Deathly Hallows - Part 1

CLEVERNESS

> ❝ **What we'd need to do is to get inside the Slytherin common room and ask Malfoy a few questions without him realizing it's us.** ❞
>
> **— HERMIONE GRANGER**
> *Harry Potter and the Chamber of Secrets*

In *Harry Potter and the Chamber of Secrets*, Hogwarts was plagued by something Petrifying students . . . and even a ghost! Harry, Hermione, and Ron were determined to find the source, and they believed Draco Malfoy could provide some information. The problem was Malfoy—a Slytherin and Harry's enemy—would not knowingly give Harry any information. Hermione's diligence and clever concoctions—along with her willingness to break "about fifty rules"—was the perfect recipe for mystery-solving. Hermione decided to brew a Polyjuice Potion, which would allow the three of them to assume the likenesses of Slytherin students. They just needed to add the students' hairs to the mixture. Even though Draco did not prove to be helpful, Harry and Ron were able to sneak into the Slytherin common room undetected.

IT HELPS TO BE CLEVER AGAINST CUNNING CREATURES

Harry called Hermione brilliant for deducing that the Sword of Gryffindor could destroy Horcruxes. "Actually, I'm highly logical, which allows me to look past extraneous detail and perceive clearly that which others overlook."

Harry Potter and the Deathly Hallows - Part 1

During Harry's battle with the Basilisk, Dumbledore's phoenix, Fawkes, swooped in to blind the creature. But the beast was still able to track Harry by sound and corner him. Harry thought fast, grabbed a rock, and tossed it past the Basilisk. The idea worked and the Basilisk followed the sound and slithered away.

Harry Potter and the Chamber of Secrets

Harry knew that a house-elf had to be freed when their master presented them with an article of clothing. To help free Dobby from his cruel masters, Harry placed a sock in Tom Riddle's diary and cleverly tricked Lucius Malfoy into giving the book to Dobby.

Harry Potter and the Chamber of Secrets

Ron and Hermione were having trouble destroying the Hufflepuff's cup, the fourth Horcrux. Then Ron realized that the skeleton of the Basilisk was still in the Chamber of Secrets where Harry had vanquished it. Since Basilisk venom could destroy a Horcrux, it only made sense that a fang from its skull would do the trick. Ron's clever idea worked.

Harry Potter and the Deathly Hallows - Part 2

LOYALTY

> " You must be the one to kill me, Severus. It is the only way. Only then will the Dark Lord trust you completely. "

— PROFESSOR ALBUS DUMBLEDORE
Harry Potter and the Deathly Hallows - Part 2

Harry saw Snape's memories and finally understood the truth about Dumbledore's death. Snape had killed his friend—not as an act of betrayal but as the ultimate act of loyalty. A curse from Gaunt's ring had already sealed Dumbledore's fate. While Snape performed magic to slow the headmaster's demise, he could not stop it. Dumbledore knew Voldemort had ordered Draco Malfoy to kill him. He also knew it would be a devastating task for the young man. By delegating the onerous deed to Snape, Dumbledore would protect Draco's soul from the stain of murder.

LOYALTY IS THE FOUNDATION OF FRIENDSHIP

Hermione stepped in front of Harry to protect him from Sirius Black, who was wanted for escaping Azkaban prison.

"If you want to kill Harry, you'll have to kill us too."

Harry Potter and the Prisoner and Azkaban

Harry, Ron, and Hermione camped in the forest to escape Voldemort's Death Eaters and to develop a strategy to destroy the Horcruxes. When Ron's anger got the best of him, he threatened to leave the group. Hermione chose to stay behind with Harry. She loved Ron but knew her loyalty had to lie with Harry at the moment because his mission to find a way to defeat Voldemort was too important.

Harry Potter and the Deathly Hallows - Part 1

Dumbledore was impressed that Harry had defeated the Basilisk. The headmaster also commended Harry for possessing the only quality that could have summoned the Phoenix, Fawkes, to his rescue. "You must have shown me real loyalty down in the Chamber," he said. "Nothing but that could have called Fawkes to you."

Harry Potter and the Chamber of Secrets

Peter Pettigrew, Remus Lupin, and Sirius Black were James Potter's loyal friends at Hogwarts. The foursome was known as "The Marauders." When James was killed for his actions against Voldemort's Dark forces, he died believing all his friends had remained loyal to him. However, that was only true of Sirius and Remus. Peter turned against his friends and led Voldemort to Harry's parents and ultimately their death.

Harry Potter and the Prisoner of Azkaban

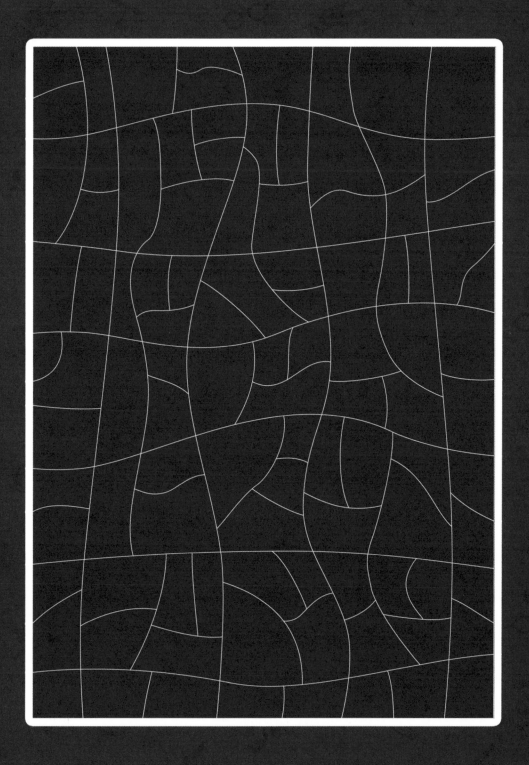

COURAGE

> " Harry's heart did beat for us! For all of us! It's not over! "

— NEVILLE LONGBOTTOM
Harry Potter and the Deathly Hallows - Part 2

Neville Longbottom was an awkward child. When Professor Trelawney predicted he would one day kill the Dark Lord, it was difficult for his classmates to picture. Neville was not famous, and he lacked Harry's natural gifts and confidence. But ultimately, he proved just as courageous as his friend. Like Harry, Neville lost both of his parents when he was young. At Hogwarts, Neville grew into a fine young man because of the support of his friends and teachers. During the Battle of Hogwarts, Neville swung the Sword of Gryffindor overhead and slashed the head off of Nagini, Voldemort's seventh and final Horcrux.

WIZARDS NEED COURAGE IN A WICKED WORLD

Despite Ron's arachnophobia, he bravely faced his fear when he followed Harry into the Forbidden Forest. There, he encountered the giant, man-eating spider, Aragog, who had a terrifying message.

"I cannot deny them fresh meat when it wanders so willingly into our midst."
—Aragog

Harry Potter and the Chamber of Secrets

In her fifth year at Hogwarts, Hermione was no longer the girl who had insisted that every rule be followed blindly. She'd grown into a young woman with the courage to defy the Ministry of Magic by founding Dumbledore's Army, a secret organization devoted to teaching students skills of Defense Against the Dark Arts. It was a dangerous undertaking during a time of spying and oppression at Hogwarts.

Harry Potter and the Order of the Phoenix

During the Battle of Hogwarts, Professor Snape brandished his wand at Harry in the Great Hall, but Professor McGonagall bravely jumped in front of him and pelted her colleague with sheets of fire. Snape fired back and retreated through the hall's large stained-glass window.

Harry Potter and the Deathly Hallows - Part 2

The first task in the Triwizard Tournament was to retrieve a golden egg protected by a dragon. Harry was unprepared and terrified. But with the help of Professor Moody, a Firebolt broomstick, and a huge dose of bravery, Harry got his egg.

Harry Potter and the Goblet of Fire

SOLUTION ON PAGE 42. STICKERS ON PAGE 64.

PROTECTION

> **I brought you here sixteen years ago, when you were no bigger than a Bowtruckle. Seems only right I should be the one to take you away.**

— RUBEUS HAGRID

Harry Potter and the Deathly Hallows - Part 1

Hagrid could barely keep from weeping the night he left infant Harry Potter on the Dursleys' doorstep. From that day forward, the enormous wizard felt a special warmth for the boy. When Harry arrived at Hogwarts eleven years later, Hagrid was determined to protect him. In *Harry Potter and the Deathly Hallows - Part 1*, Hagrid ushered Harry to safety when Voldemort was hunting for him. Hagrid took Harry on a jaw-dropping motorbike ride through London into the countryside, finally crash-landing in a stream outside the Weasleys' home.

LOVE IS THE ULTIMATE PROTECTION

One evening, Dobby the house-elf appeared in Harry's Privet Drive bedroom with a dire warning.

"Dobby has to protect Harry Potter, to warn him," he said. "Harry Potter must not go back to Hogwarts School of Witchcraft and Wizardry this year. There is a plot to make most terrible things happen."

Harry Potter and the Chamber of Secrets

Ron protected Hermione by trying to cast a spell on Draco Malfoy for calling her a "filthy little Mudblood." "Eat slugs!" Ron called out as he waved his wand. Although the spell backfired leading him to cough up slugs instead, Ron's eagerness to stand up for Hermione ultimately protected her.

Harry Potter and the Chamber of Secrets

During the Battle of Hogwarts, Bellatrix Lestrange nearly killed Ginny Weasley, provoking Mrs. Weasley's unbridled rage. "Not my daughter!" she growled at the crazed witch. Then, with the power of a mother's love and protection, she blasted Bellatrix to pieces.

Harry Potter and the Deathly Hallows - Part 2

Dumbledore arrived at the Ministry of Magic in time to defend Harry against charges of using magic while underage—specifically for using a Patronus Charm to stop Dementors from attacking him and his cousin Dudley. Dumbledore knew Harry would need protection against the tribunal, whose intentions were often questionable.

Harry Potter and the Order of the Phoenix

LEADERSHIP

> ❝ Every great wizard in history has started out as nothing more than what we are now— students. If they can do it, why not us? ❞
>
> **— HARRY POTTER**
> *Harry Potter and the Order of the Phoenix*

Teachers are leaders. When Hermione first tried to convince Harry to train Dumbledore's Army, he was reluctant. But after Hermione and others recounted Harry's death-defying trials against Dementors, the Basilisk, and other deadly creatures, Harry realized he had something to offer his peers. "Facing this stuff in real life is not like school," he told them. "In school, if you make a mistake you can just try again tomorrow. But out there when you're a second away from being murdered, or watching a friend die right before your eyes, you don't know what that's like."

LEADERSHIP IN MANY FORMS

Dumbledore understood that kindness and compassion were essential qualities in a great leader. After the upheaval surrounding the opening of the Chamber of Secrets, as well as the reemergence of the Basilisk, Dumbledore announced that all final exams had been canceled as an act of empathy toward the students. They were thrilled...all except Hermione.

Harry Potter and the Chamber of Secrets

During the First Wizarding War, Dumbledore formed the Order of the Phoenix to fight against Lord Voldemort and his Death Eaters' reign of terror. The Dark Lord was determined to take over the Ministry of Magic and to persecute Muggle-borns.

Harry Potter and The Order of the Phoenix

STRENGTH

> **" Hogwarts is threatened! Man the boundaries, protect us, do your duty to our school! "**

— PROFESSOR MINERVA McGONAGALL
Harry Potter and the Deathly Hallows - Part 2

In *Harry Potter and the Deathly Hallows - Part 2*, Professor McGonagall battled Professor Snape. The stern but kind educator with a steady demeanor and wry sense of humor was smart and strong, but she was not accustomed to being a warrior. She had to muster every ounce of her strength to lead the students and fellow teachers against Voldemort and his Death Eaters in the Battle of Hogwarts.

QUIET STRENGTH IN A TURBULENT WORLD

After Cedric Diggory's death at the hands of Voldemort, Dumbledore urged the students at Hogwarts to stick together.

"We are only as strong as we are united, as weak as we are divided."

Harry Potter and the Goblet of Fire

Harry had a natural talent as a wizard. He perfected the Patronus Charm in his third year—a spell even adult wizards struggled to master. He also knew how to deploy a Shield Charm, which he used to knock Professor Snape off his feet.

During their first flying class, Draco Malfoy grabbed Neville Longbottom's Remembrall and then took off on the broom. Showing no fear, Harry hopped on his broom and flew after Draco. In the process, he not only demonstrated strength of character, but also flying skills that made him a perfect Quiddich Seeker.

Harry Potter and the Sorcerer's Stone

When Harry first met Lucius Malfoy at Flourish and Blotts, Lucius noted the scar on Harry's forehead and boasted about the legendary status of the Dark Lord who had left the mark. This reminder of his parents' death gave Harry the strength to tell off even a powerful wizard like Lucius. "Voldemort killed my parents," Harry said. "He was nothing more than a murderer."

Harry Potter and the Chamber of Secrets

WISDOM

> ## " It is our choices, Harry, that show what we truly are, far more than our abilities. "

— PROFESSOR ALBUS DUMBLEDORE
Harry Potter and the Chamber of Secrets

Dumbledore was a philosopher at heart. His observations were remarkable reflections on life's deepest truths. After Harry defeated the Basilisk, he confided in the headmaster that he'd noticed similarities between himself and Lord Voldemort and that it frightened him. Dumbledore assuaged Harry's fears, explaining that the Dark Lord had transferred some of his powers to Harry the night he tried to kill him, but that didn't mean Harry was him. Dumbledore believed no one was ever fully at the mercy of friends, families, or surroundings. He regularly reminded Harry and the others at Hogwarts that choice and free will were keys to integrity and happiness.

WHEN A WIZARD'S WORDS ARE WISE

Mr. Weasley stood toe-to-toe with Lucius Malfoy as he hissed insults at him and his family. But Arthur was armed with a deep wisdom that left him unfazed by jabs like: "What's the use of being a disgrace to the name of 'wizard' if they don't even pay you for it?" Arthur replied: "We have a very different idea of what disgraces the name of wizard, Malfoy."

Harry Potter and the Chamber of Secrets

Dumbledore told Harry that the Sorting Hat had placed Harry in Gryffindor for a reason. He could have been in Slytherin, but the headmaster made Harry understand that the process had more wisdom behind it than Harry thought. The Hat had sorted him in to Gryffindor merely because he had the desire to ask.

Harry Potter and the Chamber of Secrets

When Professor Lupin learned that Harry's Boggart was a Dementor, he was impressed. "That suggests that what you fear the most is fear itself," Lupin said. "This is very wise."

Harry Potter and the Prisoner of Azkaban

Hermione was called "the brightest witch of her age." She actively pursued academic achievement but was wise enough to understand there was more to life than that. When Harry told her she was a better wizard than he was, she smiled, "Me? Books! And cleverness! There are more important things...friendship and bravery."

Harry Potter and the Sorcerer's Stone

DEDICATION

" Dobby is a free elf. And Dobby has come to save Harry Potter and his friends. "

— DOBBY THE HOUSE-ELF
Harry Potter and the Deathly Hallows - Part 1

After Harry secured Dobby's freedom from the Malfoy family, the house-elf permanently dedicated himself to Harry's well-being. At Malfoy Manor, when the Malfoys and sadistic Bellatrix Lestrange attacked and captured Harry and his friends, Dobby went on the offensive. He climbed a chandelier, loosened the fixture, and dropped it on Bellatrix so she would release Hermione. Next, the elf grabbed Narcissa Malfoy's wand, which would have been unthinkable when the Malfoys were his masters. "Dobby has no master," he said. "Dobby is a free elf." Acting quickly, he gathered Harry and the group and Disapparated to safety. But it was too late. Dobby's dedication cost him his life, and he was fatally wounded by Lestrange's knife.

DEDICATION TO FRIENDS AND FAMILY

Dumbledore dedicated his life to his students. "Help will always be given at Hogwarts to those who ask for it."
Harry Potter and the Deathly Hallows - Part 2

After becoming a Death Eater, Voldemort forced Draco Malfoy to murder his headmaster, Professor Dumbledore. But when Draco stood face to face with his teacher, he was overcome by Dumbledore's kindness and fought back tears as he tried to talk himself into the deed. Fortunately, Dumbledore was also devoted to his student, and he already arranged for Snape to intervene and kill him first.
Harry Potter and the Half-Blood Prince

Before their untimely death, Sirius Black promised his friends James and Lily Potter that he would take care of their child. When Sirius Black saw Lucius Malfoy holding Harry captive during the battle in the Department of Mysteries at the Ministry of Magic, he screamed, "Get away from my godson!" and then punched the Dark wizard.

Harry Potter and the Order of the Phoenix

PATIENCE

> **I'll be in my bedroom, making no noise and pretending that I don't exist.**

— HARRY POTTER
Harry Potter and the Chamber of Secrets

It was nothing short of amazing that Harry didn't explode with anger growing up in the Dursley home. His adoptive family was a particularly horrid bunch of Muggles. But Harry had an almost endless reserve of patience. Still, even when Harry tried not to make waves, things got in his way. Like the night the Dursleys had a business guest for dinner and Dobby the house-elf decided to drop by for a visit. His conversation included self-berating rants and loud head-banging. The noise could be heard throughout the house and was sure to evoke his uncle's rage. But Harry kept his cool with his annoying, but well-meaning, little visitor.

PATIENCE IS AT THE HEART OF LEARNING

Professor McGonagall summoned Harry, Ron, and Hermione to her office. "Why is it when something happens, it is always you three?" she asked with her usual mix of patience, ire, and admiration. "Believe me, Professor, I've been asking myself the same question for six years," Ron said.

Harry Potter and the Half-Blood Prince

Snape had no patience for "foolish wand waving or silly incantations." But beneath the exasperation, the former Slytherin was arguably the most patient wizard at Hogwarts. As a double agent working behind the scenes with Voldemort and his Death Eaters, Snape had to wait patiently, enduring anger and hatred, as he waited for the right moment to act.

Harry Potter and the Sorcerer's Stone

Mrs. Weasley remained patient as she coached Harry to use Floo Powder for the first time. "Mind your head... Now, take your Floo Powder... Don't forget to speak very, very clearly." But Harry did not speak clearly and ended up in Knockturn Alley rather than Diagon Alley.

Harry Potter and the Chamber of Secrets

Professor Lupin offered Harry a private lesson in the Expecto Patronus spell. Harry fainted the first time he tried the protective charm against a Boggart, which had taken shape as a Dementor. But with patient urging, he tried again and created a shield so luminous, Lupin said "...you would have given your father a run for his money."

Harry Potter and the Prisoner of Azkaban

EMPATHY

> **Things we lose have a way of coming back to us in the end, if not always in the way we expect.**

— **LUNA LOVEGOOD**
Harry Potter and the Order of the Phoenix

Luna Lovegood empathized with Harry Potter's deep sense of grief. They were friends from the moment they met feeding Thestrals. The creatures could only be seen by those who had experienced death, so Luna knew Harry was a kindred spirit. She'd lost her mother. Later in their friendship, Luna offered Harry condolences when his godfather Sirius was killed. She took Harry's hand, and, in her quiet, gentle way, chatted about lost possessions. The conversation seemed meaningless, but Harry understood her metaphor—losing a loved one is painful, but, in time, it brings transformation and surprising gifts.

IF YOU DON'T HAVE EMPATHY, WHOM CAN YOU LOVE?

Hermione was not able to watch as Defense Against the Dark Arts teacher, Professor Moody, taunted her friend Neville during the Unforgiveable Curses lesson. Neville was frozen in fear as the Death Eater disguised as Moody made him watch a huge spider writhe in pain, using the same curse as the one that drove Neville's parents to insanity. "Can't you see it's bothering him?" Hermione said, jumping to her feet. "Stop it!"

Harry Potter and the Goblet of Fire

Hermione felt for her friend Harry as he stood at the foot of his parents' tombstone. She conjured up a delicate wreath of roses to show her sympathy. Harry shed a few tears then wished Hermione a Merry Christmas. She did the same and then softly rested her head on her dear friend's shoulder.

Harry Potter and the Deathly Hallows - Part 1

Professor McGonagall rushed to comfort Professor Trelawney, who sat outside next to her suitcases and cried. Cold-hearted Dolores Umbridge had just fired the Divination teacher. McGonagall had never been fond of Trelawney, but she couldn't help but feel sorry for her eccentric colleague, who had just lost the job she loved.

Harry Potter and the Order of the Phoenix

Hermione fought back tears when Draco Malfoy called her a "Mudblood." Later, Hagrid assured her that the better-than-thou Malfoys were not worth her trouble, nor were they any better at magic than she was. They were no match for her, he told her. "Don't you think on it for one minute."

Harry Potter and the Chamber of Secrets

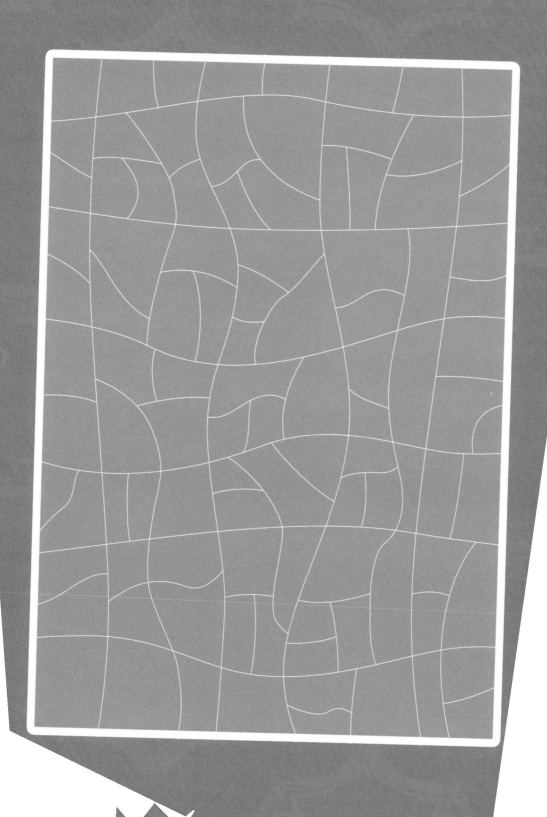

RESILIENCE

> ## " The ones who love us never really leave us. You can always find them in here. "
>
> ## — SIRIUS BLACK
> *Harry Potter and the Prisoner of Azkaban*

When Sirius Black escaped from Azkaban, he used his freedom to find his godson and tried to do some good in the world. Once he was able to convince Harry that he was innocent of the crimes with which he had been charged, he gained his trust and tried to be as much of a surrogate father as he could. Prison might have broken another man, but Sirius did his best to reclaim what he could of his life. Besides reconnecting with Harry, he made sure to expose the misdeeds of Peter Pettigrew, whom he had once called a friend.

FAILURE IS THE FIRST STEP TO STARTING OVER

During the Battle at Hogwarts, Professor McGonagall counted on Seamus Finnigan to stop Voldemort's army of Death Eaters by blowing up the wooden bridge. As a first-year at Hogwarts, Finnigan had been so bad at magic that he practically blew himself up three times. As a young man, he embraced his penchant for explosions. McGonagall suggested Neville confer with Seamus to get the bridge job done because, she recalled, "He has a particular proclivity for pyrotechnics."

Harry Potter and the Deathly Hallows - Part 2

Two Dementors trapped Harry and his cousin, Dudley, in an underground tunnel. One nearly choked Harry to death, while the other pinned the Muggle boy to the ground. Harry fended his attacker off with a Patronus Charm. When he saw Dudley fighting for his life, Harry found the resilience to reach for his wand and blast the Dark creature off him.

Harry Potter and the Order of the Phoenix

EMPOWERMENT

"I have something worth living for."

— RON WEASLEY
Harry Potter and the Deathly Hallows - Part 1

As Dementors attacked and chaos reigned at the Weasley family wedding, Hermione grabbed Ron to make an escape. Harry joined them and, in a flash, the trio Disapparated and Apparated in the middle of a busy street in London. They found a café for a moment of respite. But within seconds the friends had to pull out their wands and fight off two Death Eaters disguised as workmen. Completely on their own, the trio was now empowered to defend themselves, even in dangerous situations far from Hogwarts.

THE QUIET CONFIDENCE OF EMPOWERMENT

After Harry died at Voldemort's hand, Dumbledore greeted him and told him it was time to engage in the battle for which he'd been born. Dumbledore told Harry that the Dark Lord was no longer part of him. The last Horcrux had been destroyed and it was time to defeat Voldemort.

Harry Potter and the Deathly Hallows - Part 2

Nineteen years after the Battle of Hogwarts, a new generation of witches and wizards were empowered to begin their training at the great Scottish castle that had been home to Harry, Ron, and Hermione for so many years.

Harry Potter and the Deathly Hallows - Part 2

SOLUTIONS

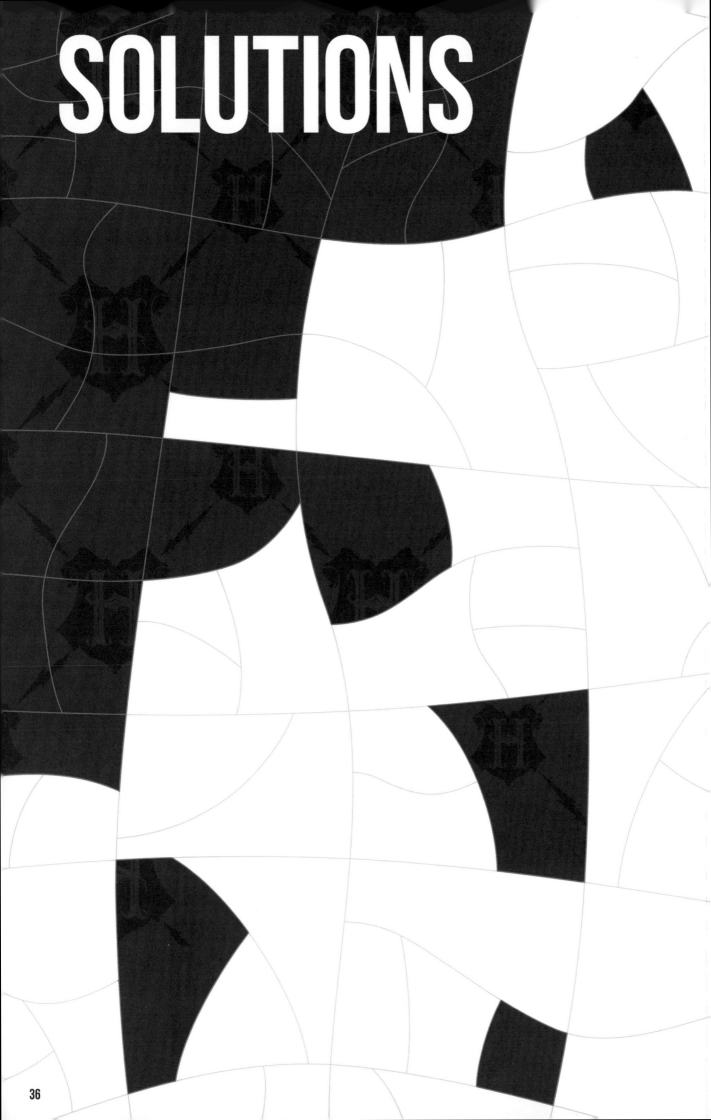

FRIENDSHIP

SELFLESSNESS

TRUSTWORTHINESS

CLEVERNESS

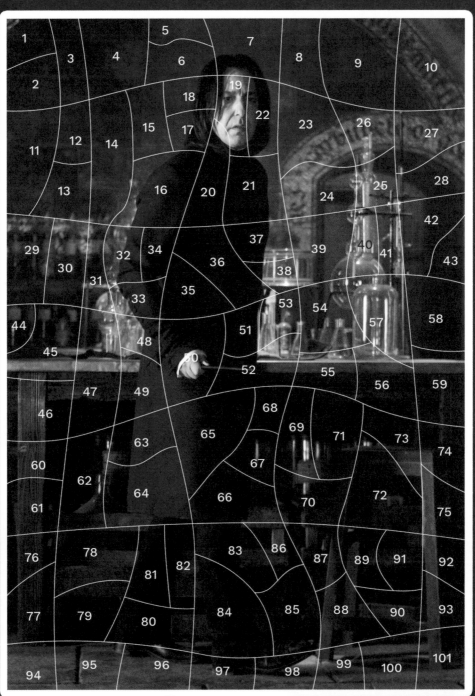

LOYALTY

COURAGE

PROTECTION

LEADERSHIP

STRENGTH

WISDOM

DEDICATION

PATIENCE

EMPATHY

RESILIENCE

EMPOWERMENT

STICKERS